HOORAY FOR
CONSTRUCTION WORKERS!

by Kurt Waldendorf

BUMBA BOOKS™

LERNER PUBLICATIONS ◆ MINNEAPOLIS

Note to Educators:

Throughout this book, you'll find critical thinking questions. These can be used to engage young readers in thinking critically about the topic and in using the text and photos to do so.

Lerner Publications Company
A division of Lerner Publishing Group, Inc.
241 First Avenue North
Minneapolis, MN 55401 USA

For reading levels and more information, look up this title at www.lernerbooks.com.

Library of Congress Cataloging-in-Publication Data

Names: Waldendorf, Kurt, author.
Title: Hooray for construction workers! / by Kurt Waldendorf.
Other titles: Hooray for community helpers!
Description: Minneapolis : Lerner Publications, [2017] | Series: Bumba books—Hooray for community helpers! | Audience: Ages 4–8. | Audience: K to grade 3. | Includes bibliographical references and index.
Identifiers: LCCN 2016001267 (print) | LCCN 2016008839 (ebook) | ISBN 9781512414417 (lb : alk. paper) | ISBN 9781512414738 (pb : alk. paper) | ISBN 9781512414745 (eb pdf)
Subjects: LCSH: Construction workers—Juvenile literature.
Classification: LCC TH159 .W35 2017 (print) | LCC TH159 (ebook) | DDC 690.092—dc23

LC record available at http://lccn.loc.gov/2016001267

Manufactured in the United States of America
1 – VP – 7/15/16

Expand learning beyond the printed book. Download free, complementary educational resources for this book from our website, www.lernerresource.com.

Table of Contents

Builders

Construction workers have many different jobs. They work together to build things.

Workers build the roads we drive on.

They make the buildings we live in.

What else do you think construction workers build?

Some workers make

things out of wood.

They use saws and drills.

They make walls and

cabinets.

Other workers build

with metal.

They weld steel.

Steel holds up tall

buildings in cities.

Plumbers add pipes.

Pipes move water.

This plumber uses a wrench to

connect pipes.

Other workers work with electricity.

They put wires into buildings.

Wires connect lights to electricity.

What else do you think needs electricity in buildings?

Workers often

work outside.

They work in the heat.

They even work in

the snow.

Workers wear helmets and gloves.

These keep workers safe.

They also wear tool belts.

Tool belts carry workers' supplies.

Why do construction workers wear tool belts?

Construction workers also take

down old buildings.

They help our community.

Construction Worker Tools

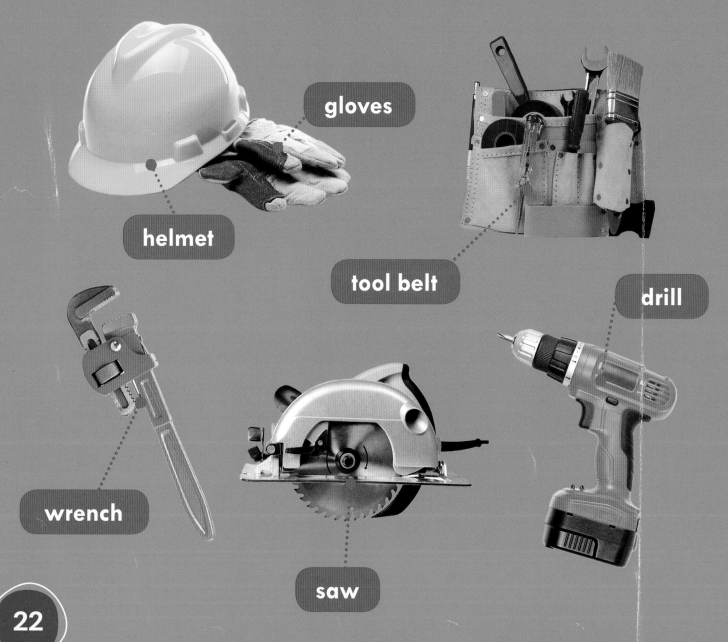

gloves

helmet

tool belt

drill

wrench

saw

Picture Glossary

electricity

power used by machines

pipes

metal or plastic tubes

tool belts

belts that hold many tools

weld

to heat and join pieces of metal

23

Index

Read More

Heos, Bridget. *Let's Meet a Construction Worker.* Minneapolis: Millbrook Press, 2013.

Jeffries, Joyce. *Meet the Construction Worker.* New York: Gareth Stevens Publishing, 2014.

Siemens, Jared. *Construction Worker.* New York: AV2 by Weigl, 2015.

Photo Credits